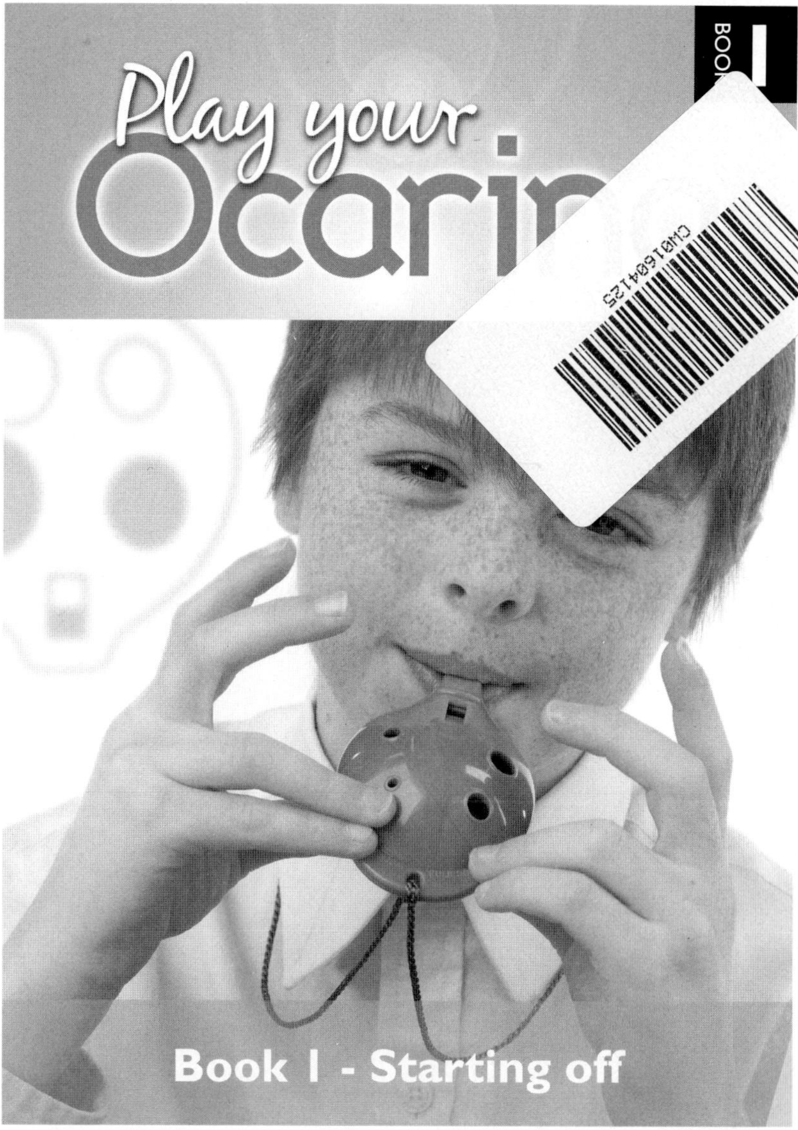

'Play your Ocarina' Book 1 First published 1992 **ISBN 1 871210 04 6**
'Play your Ocarina' Book 1 CD edition First published 2006 **ISBN 1 871210 25 9**

Contents

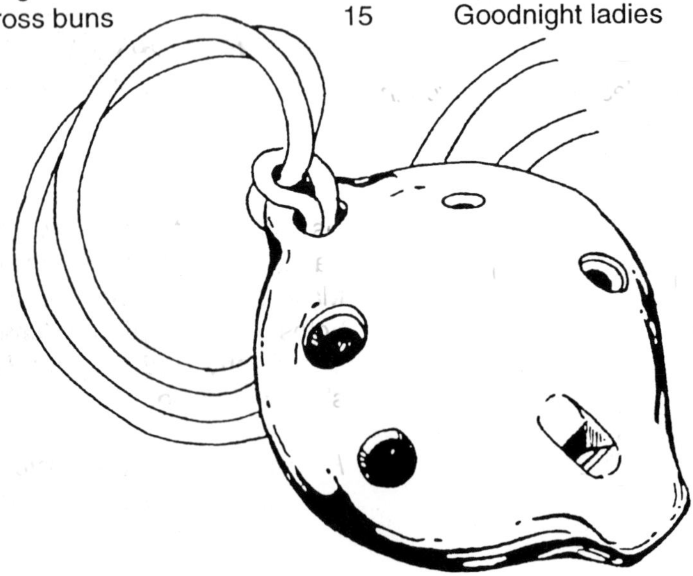

Look at your ocarina
See if you can find the string, mouthpiece, whistle-hole, finger-holes and, if you have a 6-hole instrument, the thumb-holes underneath.

Starting off

Wear your ocarina by putting the string round your neck.

Hold your ocarina so that the mouthpiece points towards you with the four finger-holes on top. Tilt the string-end down towards the ground and keep all the holes open. Place third and fourth fingers above and below the string-hole for extra support.

Breathe gently into the mouthpiece with a 'doo' movement of your tongue. Adjust the strength of your breath to produce the best sound, keeping your top lip clear of the whistle-hole.

Playing with all the holes open gives you the ***highest*** *sounding note.*

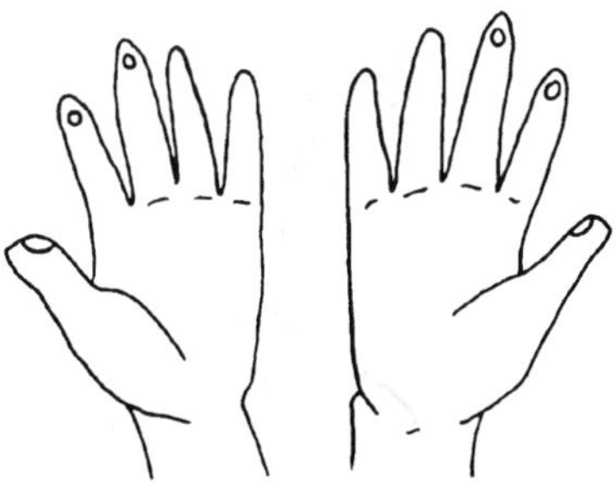

Using the first two fingers of each hand, cover all four finger-holes. Make sure these and any thumb-holes are **completely covered**. The fleshy pad of your fingers should be used.

Playing with all holes covered gives you the ***lowest*** *sounding note.*

You are now ready to play all the notes on the top 4 holes.
If you have a 6-hole ocarina, keep the thumb-holes covered **all the time** for the moment.

Oc-pix and tunes

Look at the oc-pix below to see which holes to cover for each note.
Any thumb-holes should stay covered.

Play with holes open
for high 'D'

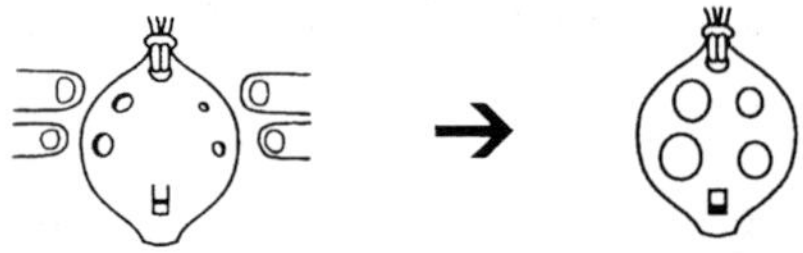

Play with 4 holes covered
for low'D'

Cover the 2 holes
nearest the mouth-piece
with your first fingers
to play 'A'

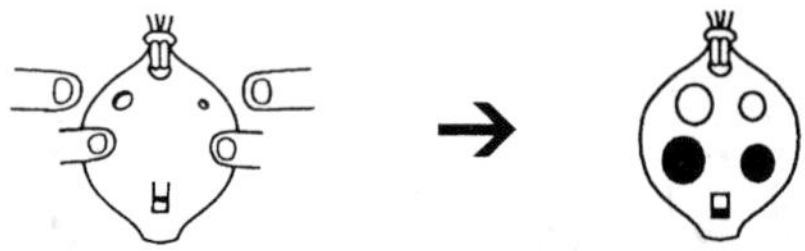

Cover the 2 larger holes
on the left to play 'G'

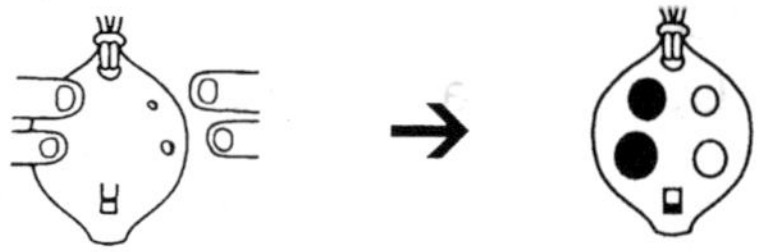

Cover the smallest hole
to play 'C#'

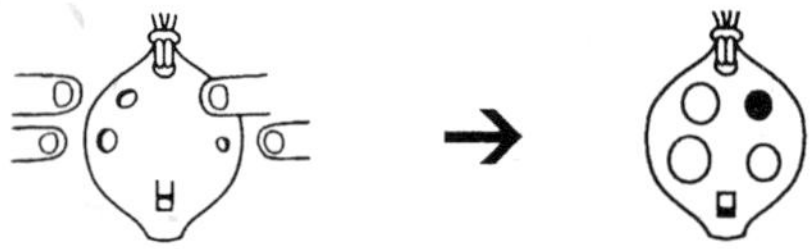

Cover all holes *except*
the smallest to play 'E'

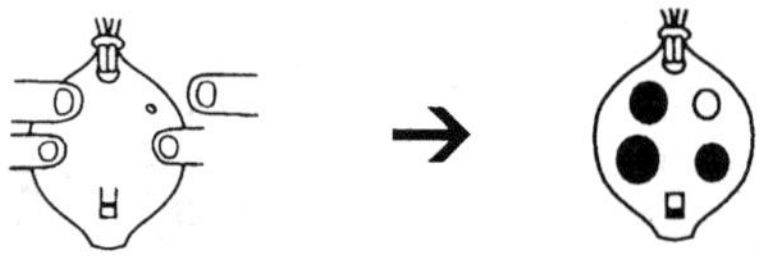

Now play the scale of D major below and the tune opposite

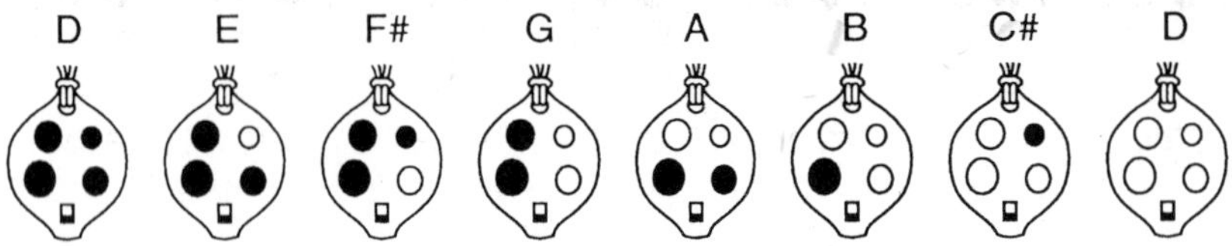

Twinkle, twinkle little star

Twin - kle, twin - kle lit - tle star,

How I won - der what you are.

Up a - bove the world so high,

Like a dia - mond in the sky,

Twin - kle, twin - kle lit - tle star,

How I won - der what you are.

Kumbaya

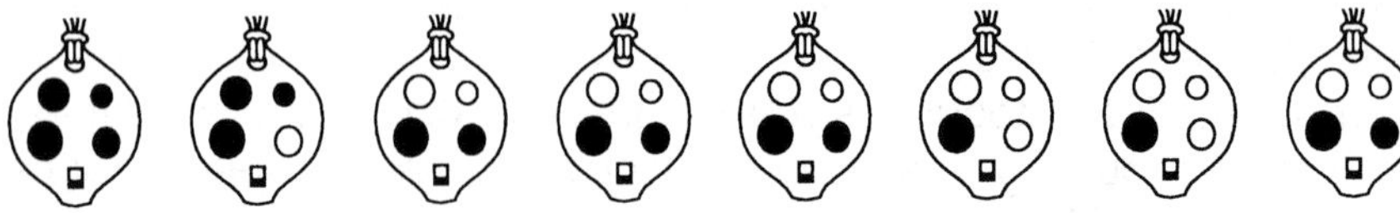

Kum - ba - ya my Lord, Kum - ba - ya
D D G D

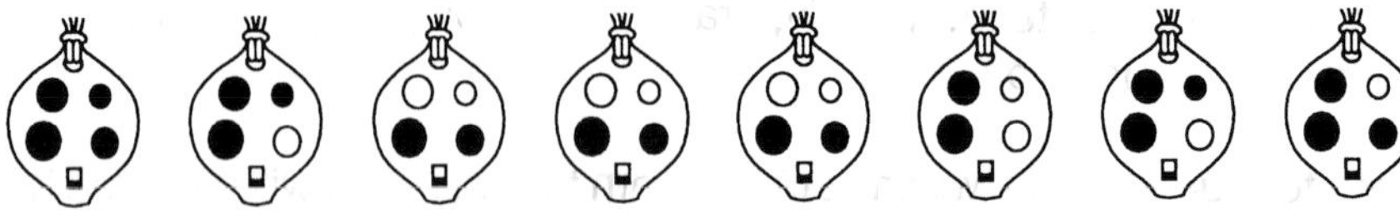

Kum - ba - ya my Lord, Kum - ba - ya
D D Em A7

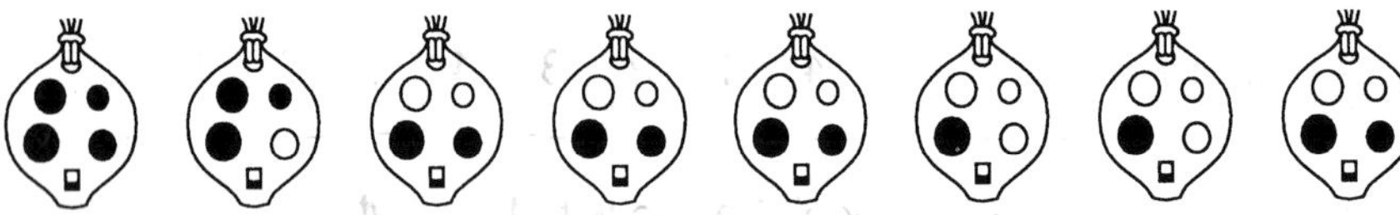

Kum - ba - ya my Lord, Kum - ba - ya
D D G D

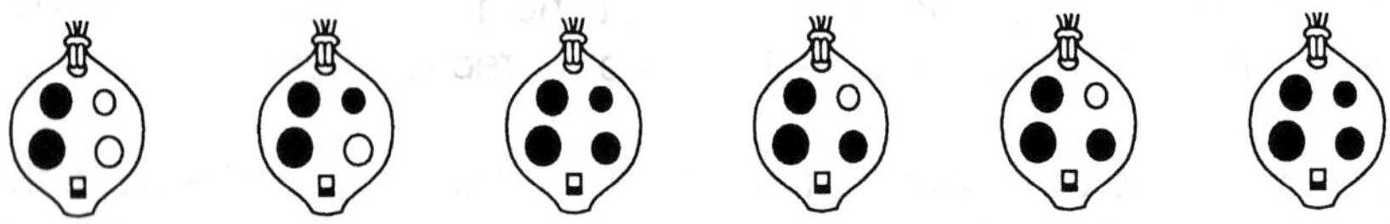

Oh Lo - rd, Kum - ba - ya
G D A7 D

The letters underneath the words give chords for guitar or other instruments. These are explained on page 15.

Starting and ending notes

To play well, you need to be able to start notes with a crisp, clean sound. Try saying 'doo' and hold the 'oo' for a few moments. Now say 'doo-doo-doo-doo' with a continuous sound. Blow steadily as you whisper 'doo-doo-doo-doo'. Repeat this last experiment as you blow steadily into your ocarina. Can you hear the separate notes that you are making on one continuous breath? This is called '**tonguing**'.

Try tonguing the rhythm of any tune as you hold down a single note. See if a friend can guess what the tune might be. Try tonguing the rhythm to 'Twinkle twinkle', 'Kumbaya' or any other tune. Finally, practise tonguing as you play the correct notes for tunes in this book.

It is best to tongue all notes when you first learn to play. This will help you to start notes cleanly. Ending notes can similarly be controlled by bringing the tongue forward to the roof of the mouth to stop the airflow.

Count 4 in your head and play different length sounds like this:

1	2	3	4	1	2	3	4	1	2	3	4	1	2	3	4
—	—	—	—	——		——		—	—	—	—	————			

Do you know which tune in this book begins with this rhythm of notes?

It is a good idea to develop your best possible sound. Play long notes. Experiment with the strength of breath that produces a warm singing tone. On some tunes, you may like to '**slur**' notes by tonguing the first and allowing your fingers to move from note to note. This only works if there are no repeated notes.

Remember to breathe deeply so that you can play more than just a few notes on a single breath. Breathe at the end of a line of music or at points where you would breathe if you were singing it as a song. If you relax as you play, you will find that very little breath is needed for playing the ocarina. Don't try too hard! Enjoy the sounds that you make and it's possible that others may enjoy them too!

London's burning

4 part round

1

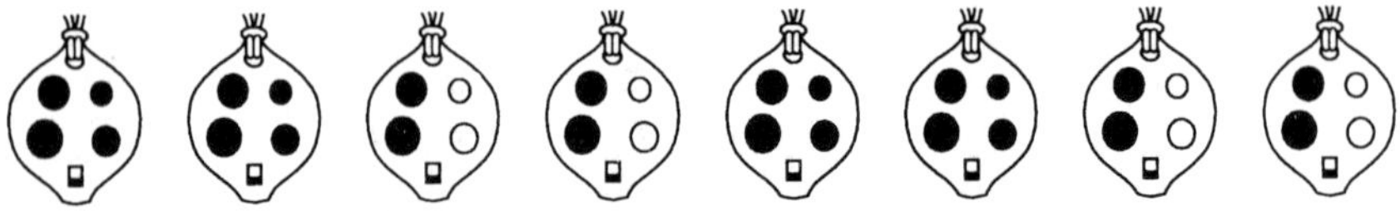

Lon - don's burn - ing, Lon - don's burn - ing,

D7 G D7 G

2

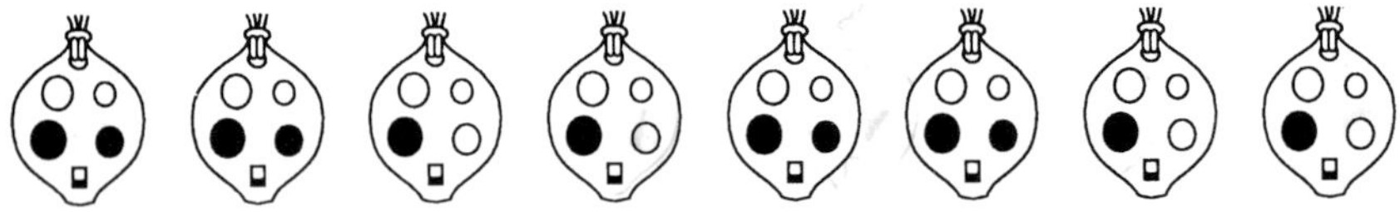

Fetch the en - gines, fetch the en - gines,

D7 G D7 G

3

Fire, fire! Fire, fire!

D7 G D7 G

4

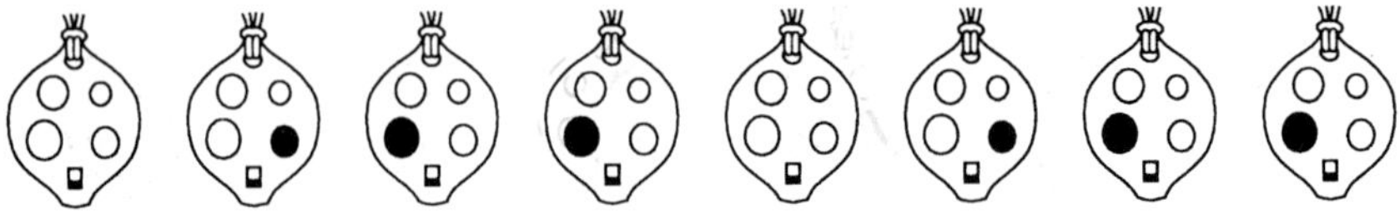

Pour on wa - ter, pour on wa - ter!

D7 G D7 G

Use your third and fourth fingers to support the string-end.
This is essential for playing top notes.

Frère Jacques

4 part round

1
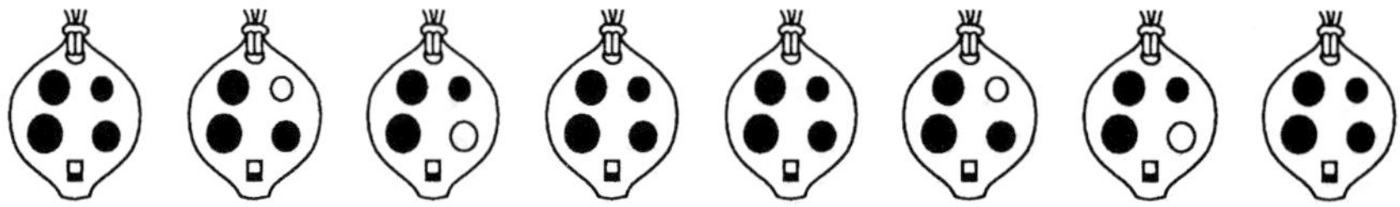

Frè - re Jac - ques, Frè - re Jac - ques,

D A7 D D A7 D

2
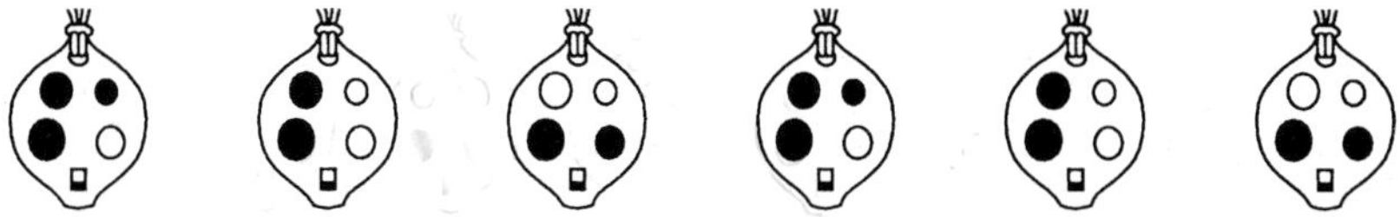

Dor - mez vous? Dor - mez vous?

D A7 D D A7 D

3
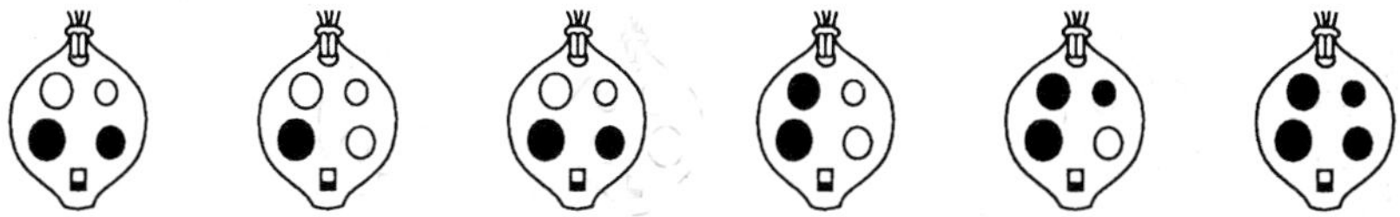

Son - nez les ma - ti - nes!

D A7 D

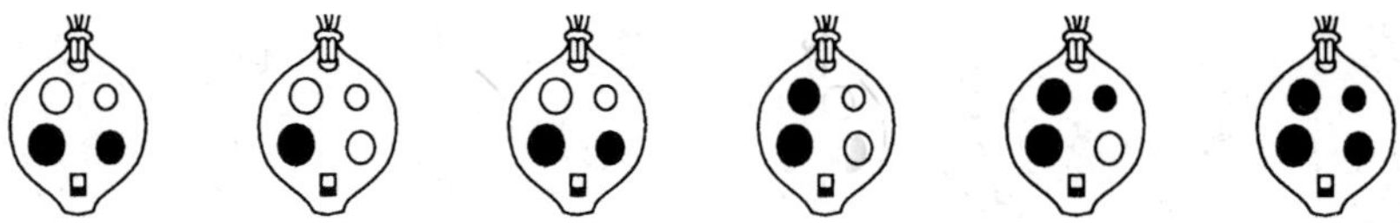

Son - nez les ma - ti - nes!

D A7 D

4
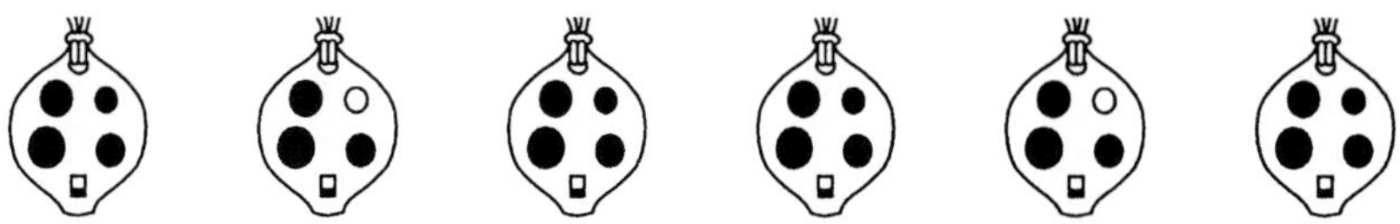

Ding, dang, dong! Ding, dang, dong!

D A7 D D A7 D

Yankee Doodle

Yan	-	kee	Doo	-	dle	went	to	town
G						G		D

A	-	rid	-	ing	on	a	po	-	ny
		G					G		D

Stuck	a	feath	-	er	in	his	cap
G					C		

And	called	it	mac	-	a	-	ro	-	ni
	D						G		

Quiz

Can you make a tune from these notes?

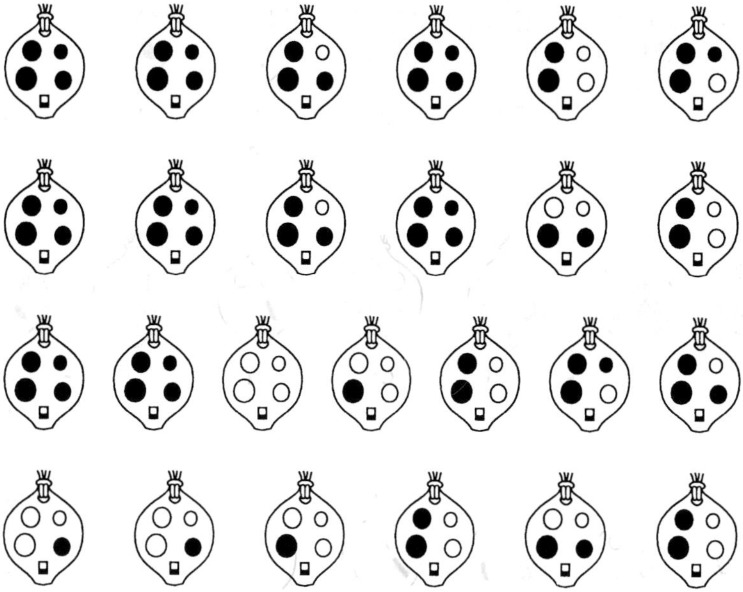

Introduction to oc-box

So far you have played tunes from oc-pix. Oc-box also show which holes to cover. Read them in the same way as oc-pix. Cover the holes which are coloured in and leave these holes open. The scale of notes below is played in the same way as the one on page 4.

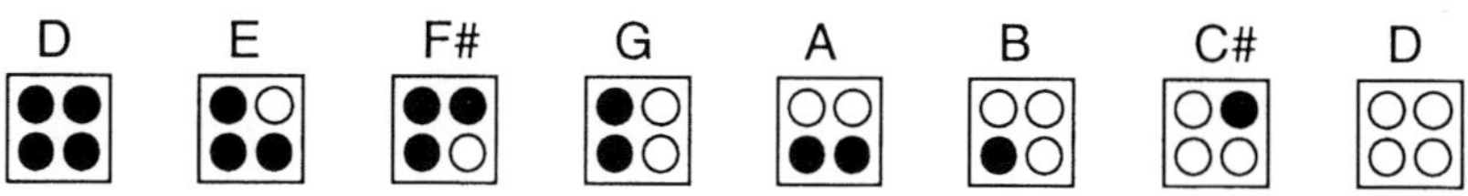

Old MacDonald

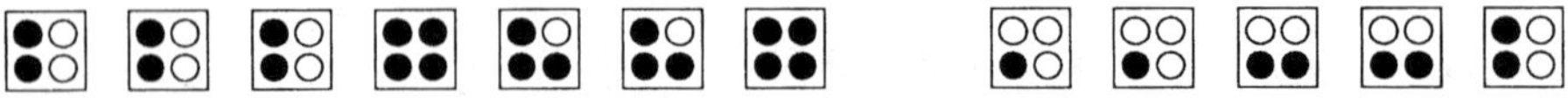

Old Mac - Don - ald had a farm, Ee - i - ee - i - o
G G C G G D G

And on that farm he had some cows, Ee - i - ee - i - o
G G C G G D G

With a moo moo here and a moo moo there
G G G G

Here a moo, there a moo, ev - 'ry - where a moo moo
C C G C

Old Mac - Don - ald had a farm, Ee - i - ee - i - o.
G G C G G D G

Jingle bells

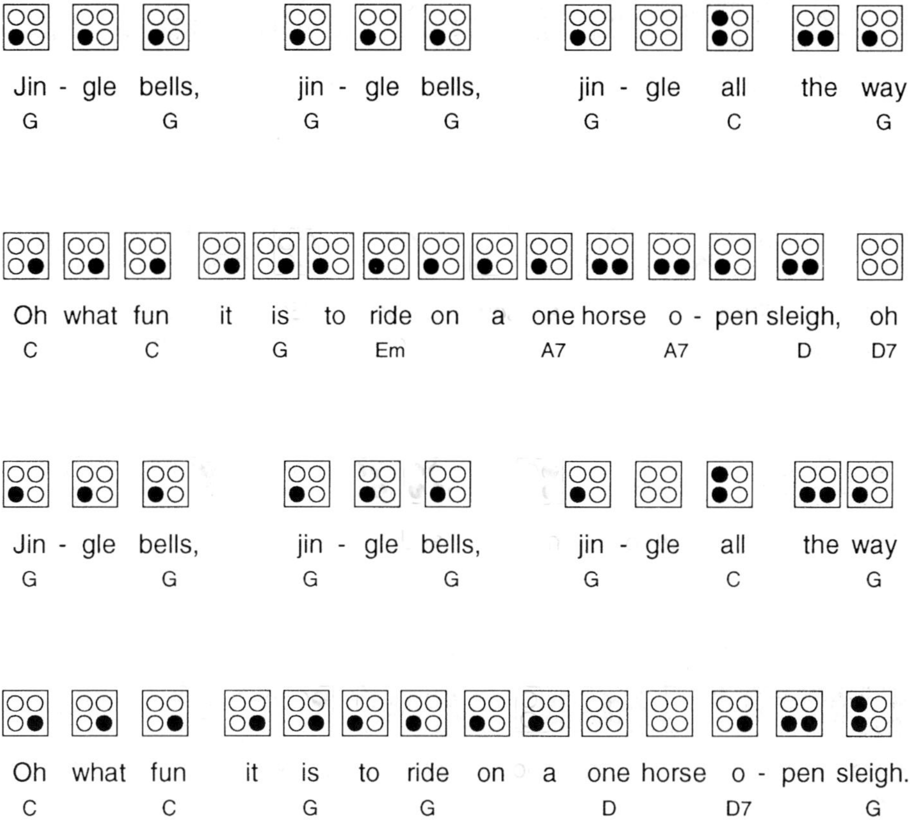

Do's and Don'ts

Do keep your ocarina clean. Sterilise it using a sterilising fluid if others play it too.
Don't allow chewing gum or anything else to block the wind-way or mouthpiece. If blocked with moisture, cover the whistle-hole and blow sharply through the mouthpiece to clear.
Do keep your ocarina safe. Wear it when playing and keep it in its box at all other times. (The ceramic ocarina may chip if roughly treated and the poly-oc may split if dropped on a hard surface.)
Don't let the string come undone or fray.
Do sit up straight when playing your ocarina.
Don't play immediately after eating.
Do cover the correct finger-holes completely so that no air can escape.
Don't eat and play at the same time.
Do experiment with the strength of your breath to produce the best sound.
Don't blow too strongly or the sound will cut out.
Do tongue notes to produce a clear, crisp tone and slur notes for gentler phrasing.
Don't blow too gently or the lowest note will sound flat.
Do support your ocarina at the string-end using your third and fourth fingers
Don't chew the mouthpiece when playing or put it too far into your mouth.
Do enjoy yourself and play for others.

Reading music

You are already reading oc-pix and oc-box, showing how to play high sounds or low sounds and others in between. Another way to show the high or low sounds is to put a note on a five line stave. This musical stave is like a ladder where notes are placed between the lines as well as on them. Play the pattern of notes below and look at the way the notes on the stave start near the top and go down to below the bottom line.

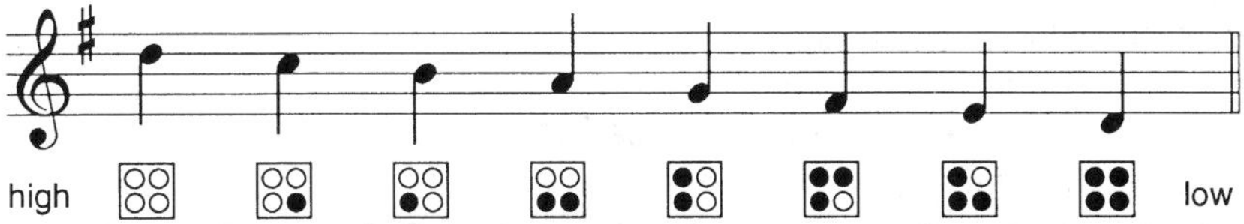

You are also reading and singing words. These give the rhythm of the music. Another way of showing rhythm is to invent different looking notes to represent long and short sounds. Look at these notes and the rhythms they make:

Play 'Hot cross buns' below. The letters above the notes give names of chords to accompany the tune. These chords may be played on guitars, keyboards, pitched percussion or autoharp. The named note may also be held by a second ocarina player as a simple accompaniment.

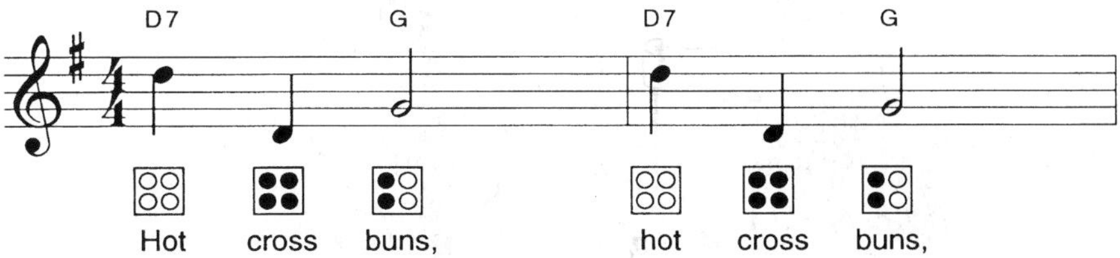

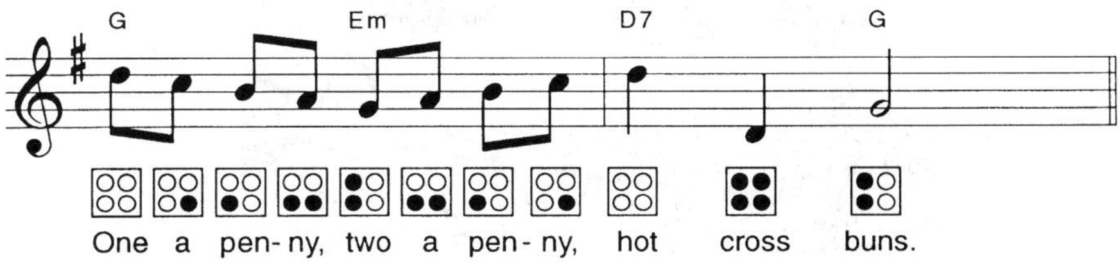

Au clair de la lune

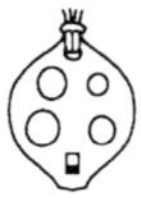

Little bird

G D7 G D
Lit - tle bird fly - ing high, you are mas - ter of the sky,
G D7 G D G
Gli - ding here, gli - ding there, o - ver fields and trees.
Am D7 G Em C D
Aer - o - planes and Con - cord too make a loud - er sound than you;
G D7 G D G
Still we hear, sweet and clear, bird song on the breeze.

Muffin man

G G Am D7
Have you seen the muf- fin man, the muf- fin man, the muf- fin man?
G G Am D7 G
Have you seen the muf- fin man who lives in Dru - ry Lane?
G G Am D7
Yes I've seen the muf- fin man, the muf- fin man, the muf- fin man.
G G Am D7 G
Yes I've seen the muf - fin man who lives in Dru - ry Lane.

Bobby Shaftoe

Oh Susanna

Stephen Foster

Stephen Foster (1826-1864) was an American who wrote many popular and sentimental songs depicting life in the southern states during pre-civil war days.

Camptown races

Stephen Foster

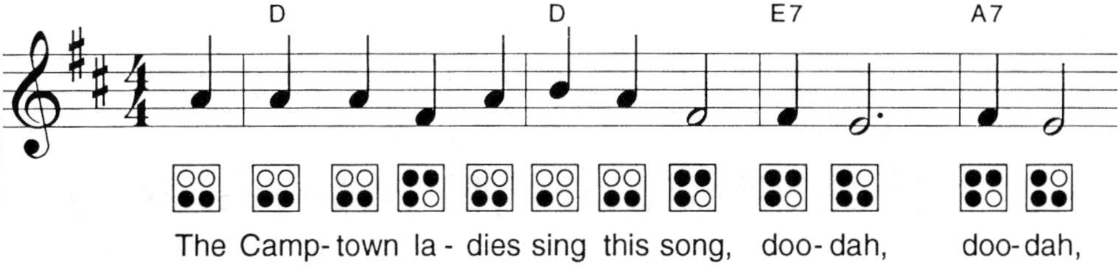

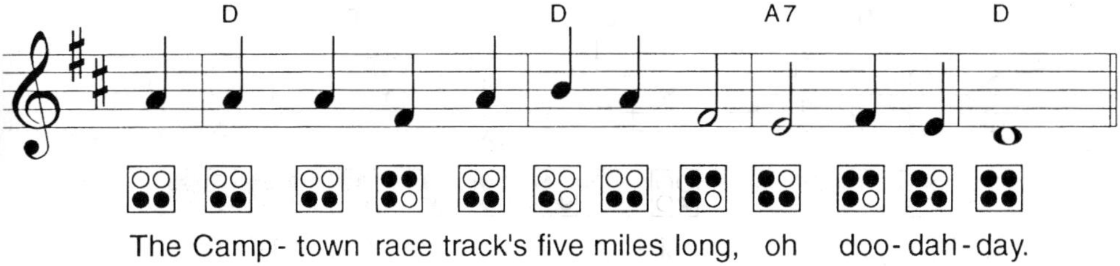

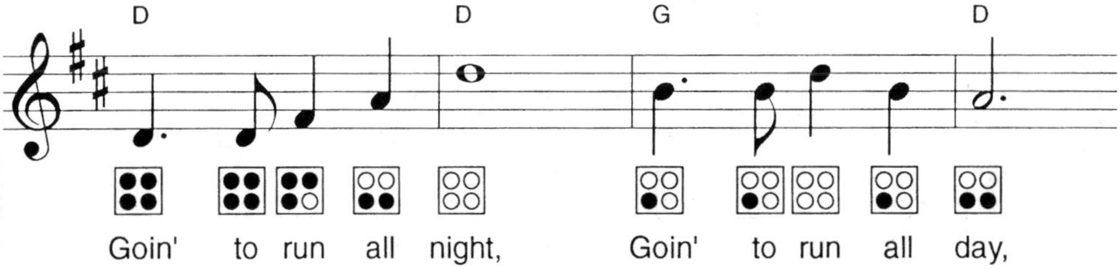

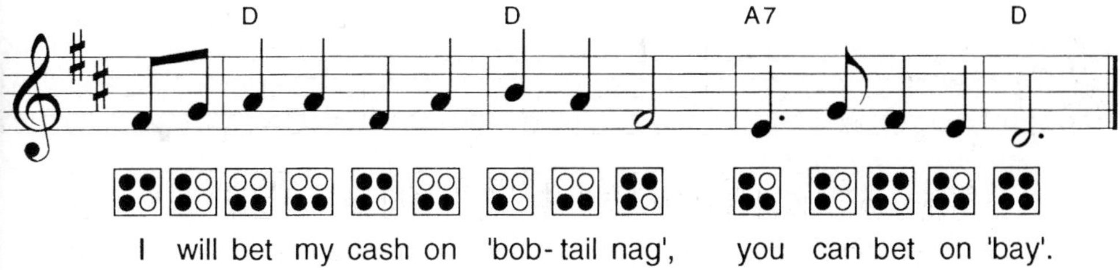

Try playing these two tunes as a medley continuing from page 20 to 21 and back to 20 without a break. Play similar medleys on pages 16 to 17 and 18 to 19.

New notes

The scale of 'D' major has eight notes and appears on pages 4 and 11. In tunes with only one sharp (the key of 'G'), the note 'C natural' (C) replaces 'C sharp' (C#) and the first hole on the right is covered instead of the smallest hole.

So far you have played all nine notes mentioned above. Two other notes are also easy to play on the top four holes of your ocarina.

'G sharp' (G#) which is also sometimes called 'A flat' (A♭)

'A sharp' (A#) which is more often known as 'B flat' (B♭)

The keyboard below shows how notes can have more than one name:

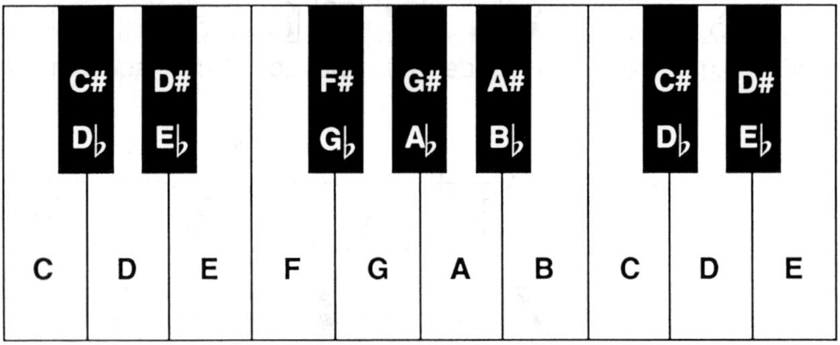

On a 6-hole ocarina it is possible to play all the notes shown on the keyboard above. The top 4 holes of Langley ocarinas give a total of 11 notes that are all as easy to play as each other. These are listed inside the back cover. The other notes that can be played on 4-hole and 6-hole ocarinas are introduced in book 2.

Practise the two 'new' notes, G# and A#, by playing the tune opposite. Look out for these notes to appear in later books in this series.

All things bright and beautiful

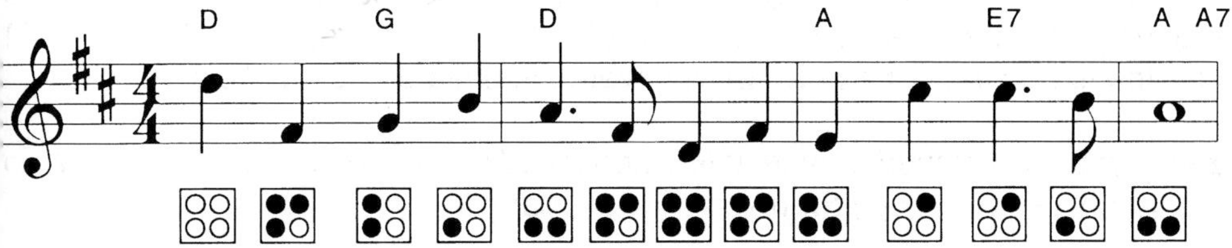

Chorus: All things bright and beau - ti - ful, all crea - tures great and small,

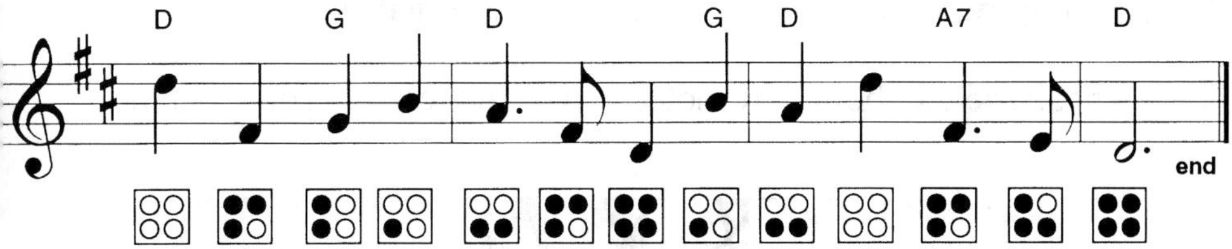

All things wise and won- der- ful, the Lord God made them all.

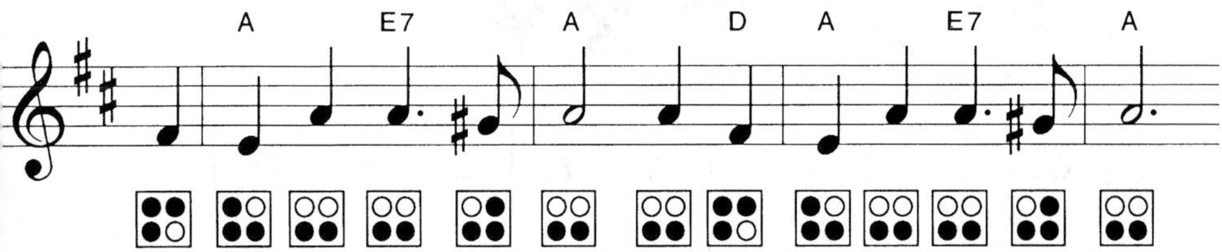

Verse: The pur - ple head - ed moun - tain, the ri - ver run - ning by,

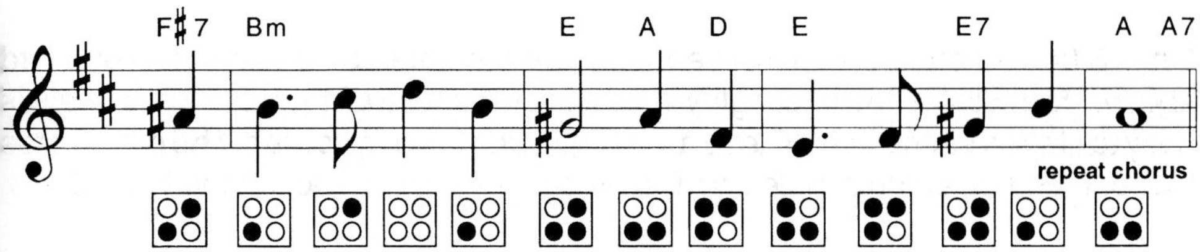

The sun - set and the mor- ning that brigh- tens up the sky:

This well loved Victorian hymn tune has a chorus in the key of 'D' and verse in 'A' giving you plenty of practice in playing the new notes introduced opposite.

Pastoral

Beethoven

Ludwig Van Beethoven (1770-1827) composed this simple melody as part of his 6th symphony, known as the 'Pastoral'. It was first performed in 1808.

Plaisir d'amour

Martini

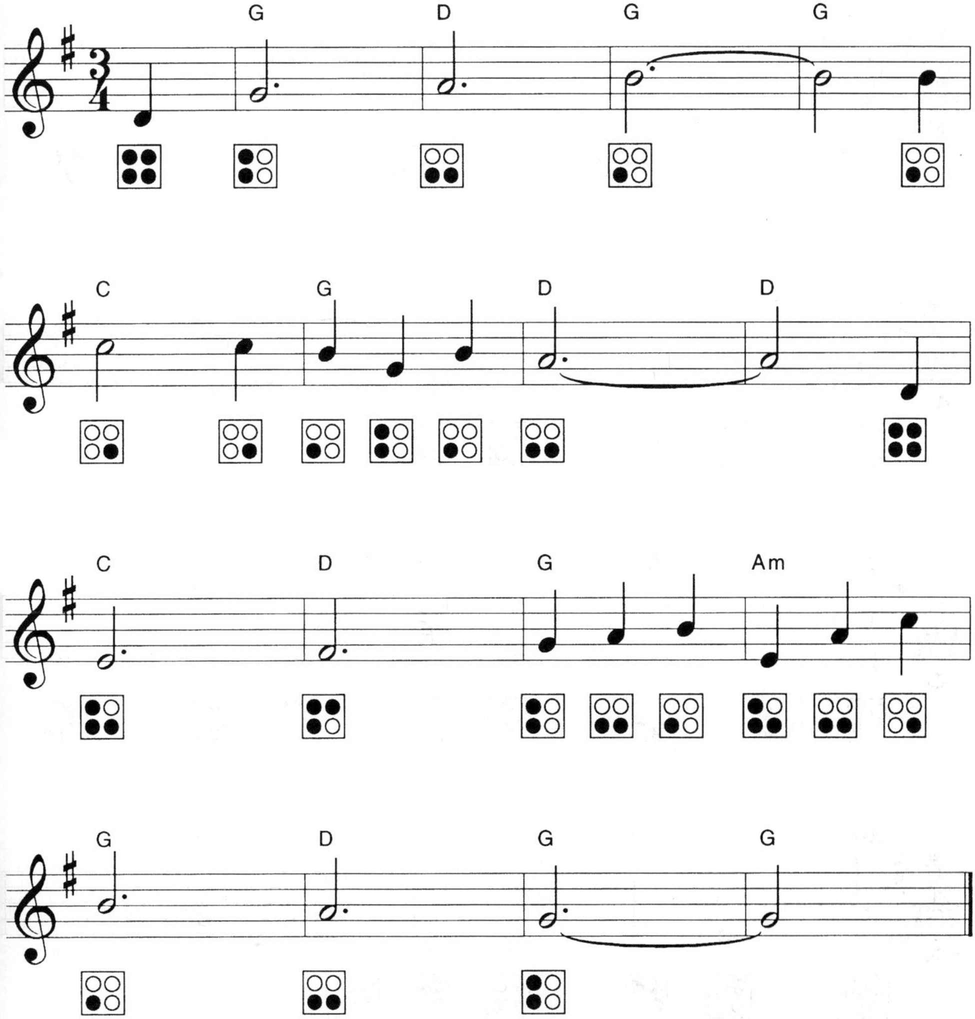

Padre Giovanni Battista Martini (1706-1784) was an Italian monk, music teacher and composer. Among his more notable students were J.C.Bach and Mozart.

New World

Dvorák

Antonin Dvorák (1841-1904) was a Czechoslovakian composer who wrote this melody for his 'New World' Symphony in 1893 after visiting New York.

Ode to joy

Beethoven

Beethoven's 9th Symphony includes this powerful tune played by orchestra and sung by soloists and choir. It has become the European 'National anthem'.

"Daisy, Daisy"

Harry Dacre

Ties at the end of the 2nd and 4th lines above join two notes together to make one long sound. Other ties appear on pages 24, 25, 27, 29, 30 and 31.

This well known Victorian music hall song is popular with people of all ages. Enjoy playing it to a steady three beats per bar waltz rhythm.

Skye boat song

Miss Annie MacLeod heard this tune sung as she sailed from Torran to Loch Coruisk in 1879. Slur phrases to suggest the gently ebbing and flowing tide.

Em
Em
Am
Am
Em
C
Em
Em
G
G
Am
Am
Em
C
Am
D
repeat first section

Goodnight ladies